Graduation
May 2010

To: Stephanie

In Christian Love!

Margaret Aldridge

Proverbs 3:5, 6

The Dream Giver for Teens

THE
DREAM
GIVER
for
TeenS

JESSICA WILKINSON
WITH BRUCE WILKINSON

Multnomah® Publishers *Sisters, Oregon*

THE DREAM GIVER FOR TEENS
published by Multnomah Publishers, Inc.
Based on *The Dream Giver* by Bruce Wilkinson
and David and Heather Kopp.
© 2004 by Exponential, Inc.
International Standard Book Number: 1-59052-459-4

Published in South Africa by Lux Verbi.BM

Unless otherwise indicated, Scripture quotations are from:
The Holy Bible, New King James Version © 1984 by Thomas Nelson, Inc.

Other Scripture quotations are from:
The Message © 1993, 1994, 1995, 1996, 2000, 2001, 2002
Used by permission of NavPress Publishing Group

Multnomah is a trademark of Multnomah Publishers, Inc.,
and is registered in the U.S. Patent and Trademark Office.
The colophon is a trademark of Multnomah Publishers, Inc.

Printed in the United States of America

For information:
MULTNOMAH PUBLISHERS, INC. · P. O. BOX 1720 · SISTERS, OR 97759

Library of Congress Cataloging-in-Publication Data

Wilkinson, Jessica.
     The dream giver for teens / Jessica Wilkinson ; with Bruce Wilkinson.
        p. cm.
     ISBN 1-59052-459-4
     1. Christian teenagers—Religious life.   I. Wilkinson, Bruce. II.
Wilkinson, Bruce Dream giver. III. Title.
     BV4531.3.W554 2004
     248.8'3—dc22

                            2004015519

        04 05 06 07 08 09—10 9 8 7 6 5 4 3 2 1 0

This book is for every teen who holds on to the
hope that life is able to take them places they
are afraid to even dare dream of.
May you find your dream, embrace it,
and change the world because of it.

I know words will never be enough to thank my family
for all they have done, but I hope you know how grateful
I am to God for giving you to me. Your belief in me has
pushed me to build wings and fly, though most would
think it impossible. Thanks for not letting me simply take
their word for it, but instead encouraging me to test it for
myself until I find that it is possible. Thank you for
chasing your dreams so passionately and leaving
footprints in the sand along the way for me to follow.

Most of all, Dream Giver, thanks for giving me a dream
far too big for me to hold on my own.

contents

No two **hearts** hold the same dream, and each heart beats to the **unique** **rhythm** of the **dream** inside it

there must be more
than this

"Welcome to Dreamland's magic carpet ride! Please climb aboard your personal flying carpet. Try to ignore the talking parrot, begin rubbing the old lamp located in the right corner of the seat pocket in front of you, and hold on tight! Your very own large blue genie, with a voice much like Robin Williams, will be with you in just a moment with the answers to all your questions as well as the ability to let you see into your future and reshape it to create the life of your dreams. But before you do, I must warn you that when dreams come true, your life will never ever be the same...but then again, that's the point of dreams, isn't it? We hope you have a pleasant experience and enjoy your stay with us!"

What would you do if that situation could take place in real life and not only in your imagination? What would you do if you had the ability to see what God wanted your life to look like, or if you could look at your dreams through eyes of understanding and not of confusion? Would things be different? If you understood your heart a little more, do you think your life would have more meaning and less frustration? Do you think your life would look a lot different than it does now? Would you be willing to follow your heart more and let it take you out of the ordinary and into the extraordinary? What would you do if I told you that it doesn't take a magic flying carpet to get you there? A life full of meaning and dreams begins just inside of you, actually—a little to the left, in what we call the heart. Interested? There may not be any talking parrots, but there will be excitement, passion, and contentment, and if you look hard enough, you just may find that life that God created you to live. Keep on reading and hold on tight. The ride is only just beginning!

I'm almost entirely convinced that every single person in the world believed that they were invincible when they were a kid. In fact, I don't think I've ever met a little kid who didn't believe that wholeheartedly. Boys make their belief in it a bit more obvious by trying to fly off couches and tables, but deep down we all thought we were secret superheroes with the ability to change the world without getting hurt. Worst-case scenario was that we might need a Band-Aid after we saved the world.

But then the day comes when we wake up, and out of nowhere something known as reality hits us. And it hits us hard! We discover that we aren't invincible, that we aren't actually superheroes, and that worst of all, we can't even really fly! Our eyes are suddenly opened to the fact that, whether we like it or not, we don't live in a world of fairy godmothers and things aren't fixed with a wand and a magic saying. In our world, most people don't even live "happily ever after"—they just live. Every day we do the same things, over and over and over again. We are taught to forget about fantasies of wild adventures and thoughts of saving the world, and instead begin studying stuff like how many animals are left in a field when all the sheep are taken away from the cows. We forsake our dreams and learn to live without the one thing that used to be our very life.

But what if I told you that it's not supposed to be this way? What if I told you that life isn't meant to be lived apart from dreams, but for them? What if I told you that your dream of saving a little bit of the world just may be what's supposed to come true, and even though you won't be someone's hero by flying across the sky, you just may be their hero by using what God put inside of you—if you find it, that is.

I used to think that living a dream was only for special people who had done something right and had somehow captured the glance of God. My theory then changed, and I began to believe that dreams were nothing more than a feeble attempt to escape reality for a while—that in order to keep going, we tell ourselves the lie that someday life will be better and we will be happier. But we don't usually do anything with our dreams except think about them, and so they don't change anything. I became certain that dreams come true only in Disney movies.

I always thought it was kind of odd how animated movies always ended at the perfect moment when the heroine's dreams finally came true. Not that any kid would want a movie to end with the heroes getting eaten by monsters, but Disney movies always seemed to end before "real life" began. Cinderella ended when she rescued the prince from a life of bachelorhood and drove off with him in a white carriage. Snow White awakened to a handsome prince kissing her, and that was where the movie stopped. No one ever told us what happened when Cinderella woke up the next morning to discover that Prince Charming had the worst morning breath imaginable. No one told us that Snow White snored when she wasn't in a coma. What happens then? Does finding your dreams mean that you will be happy forever, or just for a little while?

Like so many people in this world, I began to doubt that dreams could ever come true. And you know what? I was right. Perfect fairy-tale dreams don't come true, just as mice don't turn into horses and carry a princess in a carriage that was once a pumpkin. Fairy-tale dreams don't come true because we don't live in a world of magic. But real dreams can come true—if you listen to your heart long enough to hear the dream and pursue it.

A sad thing happens to most of us as we grow up: We start ignoring our heart when it speaks to us of our dreams. We use the distractions of life to muffle the voice of our heart, telling ourselves that we shouldn't hope for something that has no way of ever coming true. Pretty soon our dreams are locked away and then the worst thing of all happens—our heart stops talking to us. We look in the mirror one day and realize that we are almost adults and we still have no idea what we want to be when we "grow up." We're baffled by the question that we could answer when we were five! Maybe becoming a superhero isn't too realistic, but at least we had an answer. We've changed too much from that little kid who bounced around the room in a Spider-Man costume, and somehow along the way, we have forsaken the deepest part of who we are.

But as long as you're still alive, chances are pretty good that your heart is still beating. As long as you have that, you still have hope and you can still reach for your dreams. And reaching those dreams was exactly what you were created to do.

After God created the heavens and the earth, the Bible says He created humans, male and female, "in His image." Though both male and female were made in His image, He made them different. (Just thought I'd point that out in case you hadn't noticed yet!) Guys display the authority and strength of God, while girls display His purity and gentleness. Every single person God has made since the beginning of time has displayed a slightly different picture of Him—different from all the millions of people before and all the people not yet born. No speck of gold in a person's brown eyes is the same as in someone else's. But God didn't stop at outward appearances. He kept going.

> Your dream is given to you to **drive** you toward the life you were **created** to love

Within each of us He formed a heart different from every other. Inside that heart He placed a beautifully and intricately shaped dream that would make that person's heart beat. No two hearts hold the same dream, and each heart beats to the unique rhythm of the dream inside it. What can impassion one heart can leave another entirely unaffected. And it's supposed to be like that. Your dream is given to you to drive you toward the life you were created to love. No two people have the same dream, because no two people were created to live the same life. If you never go looking for your dream, you may find yourself just watching people who are chasing theirs. You may even try and chase *their* dream for a while, somehow trying to make it your own. But it won't fit inside your heart, because whether you know it or not, your own dream is already in there.

I remember when I first played the Xbox game Halo. That was one of the first times I really knew what it felt like to have no idea where I was going or what I was doing. I would somehow end up in small confined spaces while carrying a big grenade launcher. So every time I shot at the bad guy I ended up killing myself instead. It was pathetic! I had no clue what my mission was or what the whole of the landscape looked like, so I just ran around in circles the entire time, hoping that the people I was playing with wouldn't notice. And hoping that the best friend I was teamed up with wouldn't decide to get a new best friend because I was so horrible. The game would have been so much easier if I had known what I was supposed to do, how to do it, and where I was supposed to go.

Sometimes life feels like that—like we are randomly running around with no idea what we're doing or where we're supposed to go. We wake up some mornings wondering what exactly we are living for, and fall asleep many nights silently thinking, *There must be more to life than this.*

And there is. It's called your dream. It's that longing within your heart that is meant to help you find your way in life. This book was written to help you find that dream and pursue it so that life won't be anything like my completely frustrating Halo experience.

You may be a little skeptical right now. You're probably thinking that the idea that everyone has a dream seems a little too idealistic. I thought that for a while, too. Everyone does. The tragic thing is when people never stop thinking it.

I promise that if you keep reading, I will try my best to show you that every heart holds a dream inside. This book isn't going to be a bunch of "what ifs." But it is intended to explain the why, how, and what. It will explain why God placed a dream in your heart, how you find your dream, and what to expect along the path as you try to reach it. Because whether you know your dream, have forgotten it, forsaken it, ignored it, lost faith in it, or tried to kill and bury it, it's still there. Even if you don't know what it looks like, it's still there.

Let me give you a quick outline of the book so you know what to expect. In the first few pages, there's a short story about a bug that will give you the big picture of the journey that most dreamers and their dreams go through. The seven chapters that follow the story will take a deeper look at each of the seven stages on the way to your dream. We'll take a look at:

1. How to discover your dream and why it's so important to follow it.
2. Why dreams take us out of our places of comfort and safety and drive us into the unknown.
3. What to do when your dream meets opposition from the people around you.
4. How a time of testing and struggle fits into God's plan for your dream.
5. Why it's important to grow more in the One who gave you the dream, and how surrendering your dream to Him can affect the final outcome.
6. The true purpose of obstacles in your path and how to overcome them.
7. How to reach your full potential, achieve your dream, and live out the life you were created by God to adore.

This book isn't going to give you some magical formula that will make your fairy-tale dreams come true. I can't turn pumpkins into carriages and wake people out of comas by kissing them. (And I'm pretty sure that you can't either!) But I can tell you what God's heart intended when He placed our dreams inside us, and how they are meant to fit into our lives. I can help you get back a part of that little wannabe superhero that was never meant to be lost. I can help you find that heart of wild dreams you thought you had lost long ago. Your dream can become a reality. It can lead you to places you wouldn't have dared to hope for. It can lead you to the life you've always longed to live. And maybe, just maybe, in that life your dream takes you to, you will find your own "happily ever after."

Your dream can become
a reality

This story is about **Ernie**, a little gray **caterpillar**

a bug's
story

Long ago, deep within the jungles of a land far, far away, there lived a massive, ferocious, fire-breathing, human-eating dragon. But this particular story isn't about the dragon, though he does sound pretty impressive.

This story is about Ernie, a little gray caterpillar.

From the outside, there really didn't appear to be anything special about Ernie. He was an ordinary-looking bug with an ordinary-looking family. They lived in an ordinary house, and instead of boring you describing every ordinary detail of their ordinary lives, I'll just tell you that almost everything they had or did or even thought about doing was—you guessed it—*ordinary*.

Ernie and his ordinary family all lived in the Big Tree on a small island where ordinary caterpillars lived. The island wasn't beautiful, but it was nice enough. The Big Tree was the only tree on the small island, and it had provided food for all the caterpillars for as long as any of them could remember. The caterpillars' lives completely revolved around the Big Tree. In the summer they spent all their time gathering leaves so they would have enough to eat during the winter. And in the winter they spent most of their time in their homes inside the Big Tree.

The caterpillars had two goals in life: to eat and to get as ridiculously fat as possible. They were also known for their predictability, which the caterpillars prided themselves in. Inside the tree they had carved out the rather ungainly motto, "It's better to be safe, alive, and comfortable than to be adventurous, dead, and eaten by ants—which definitely isn't comfortable!" And that pretty much sums up the attitude of ordinary caterpillars.

Each morning Ernie awoke and began gathering his share of leaves for the family. Then he ate, did his chores, ate, went to the school for ordinary bugs, ate, came home, ate, did his ordinary homework, ate, and went to bed. Every day was pretty much the same for Ernie, as it was for every other caterpillar he knew on the small island. Sometimes Ernie's fat, fuzzy best friend Steve, who was the pride of his family for succeeding so well at the two goals of a caterpillar, would come over and do homework with Ernie. But it would be fair to say that life was kind of dull and ordinary. Because, you see, no one had ever told Ernie to expect more. And so he didn't.

Every day at bug school the older bugs would teach the younger bugs about the world beyond their island—though none of them had ever been there, of course. They would show the young bugs pictures of big, scary monsters and tell them of all the dangers lurking outside their small safe island. All the bugs had learned early not to show curiosity and ask about the outside world. Asking those kinds of questions was like signing yourself up for cruel and unusual punishment and was definitely not worth it. If one of them were to let his curiosity show, however, the teachers would inform the bug's parents and set up meetings with even more scary pictures for the bug to look at while his parents sat there wailing, "We're going to lose our baby bug! He's going to be eaten by monsters and die! Our poor baby bug!"

So the bugs learned not to be curious, and if ever they were, they learned to ignore their curiosity. A funny thing happened when they ignored their curiosity for a while: They found that it no longer bothered them not to know. Usually, that is.

❧

A few years passed and this little Ernie grew up—which is usually what happens when a few years pass. He graduated from the ordinary bug school at the top of his class and took a job working at the leaf report factory where most ordinary caterpillars worked. Ernie was exactly like all the other bugs and expected to be so for the rest of his short caterpillar life.

Then one day, everything changed.

Ernie woke up one Monday morning at exactly 6:45, just as he did every morning. Only something inside of him was different. He awoke to a strange stirring in his heart, and Ernie suddenly realized that deep inside he wanted more than this ordinary life. He wanted to do more than submit reports about leaves and eat all day. And for some reason, he felt as if he was *supposed* to be doing more than that—he just didn't know what.

Ernie gazed longingly out his window and wondered what life beyond the small island was really like. Glancing over at his clock, he realized he would be late for work if he didn't hurry. He quickly stuffed these strange new feelings away and went to work. All day long Ernie tried not to think about wanting more, or about wanting to *be* more. He tried to convince himself that this ordinary life was all there was. He even tried to convince himself that he was *happy* with the way things were, even though he knew he wasn't. Not at all. Not even a little.

That night, as Ernie drifted off to sleep, he wondered what it was that he was supposed to be doing. Eating and

getting fat were fun, but something was definitely
missing. Something big. When Ernie woke up the next
morning, he could take it no longer. He made up his mind
to go see the (*gasp!*) notorious Kraunk.

Kraunk was known all over the island for talking bugs
into abandoning the Big Tree and venturing into the wild,
unknown lands beyond. Parents feared him, and teachers
warned their students about him. But Ernie thought that
maybe, just maybe, Kraunk might be able to help him
figure out these strange new feelings. And so Ernie ran off
as fast as all his little legs would carry him.

Kraunk lived on the far side of the island among those who
were considered "bad" or "unordinary bugs." Ernie had
never been to that side of the island before, but he found
his way just fine. All he had to do was follow the signs that
said, "This way to the bad and unordinary bugs. We
recommend, though, that you turn around and go home!"

Kraunk didn't look half as scary as Ernie expected. In
fact, he even looked kind of friendly. . . kind of. He
opened his door wide and invited Ernie into his home.

The young caterpillar's face was clearly disturbed as
he entered. Kraunk had seen this look many times before
on the ordinary bugs of the island, especially the
caterpillars. Kraunk sat Ernie down and told him a story

that began, "Not long ago, and not far from this island…"
It was the story of an ordinary caterpillar that turned into
a butterfly. Ernie had heard about such things, but he had
been told by his ordinary friends that only a very special
breed of caterpillars ever transformed into butterflies.
Was it possible he had been told wrong? Could it be that
this was what was missing from his life? Could it be that
ordinary caterpillars were created to become more than
just ordinary? His heart leapt at the thought!

Ernie returned home that night with a jumble of
thoughts racing through his mind. Kraunk had told Ernie
that he wanted more from life because there was *supposed
to be* more to life. He also said that if Ernie decided to
become a butterfly, everything he needed was already
inside him.

He went to sleep thinking about Kraunk's words, and
when he woke up it was there, just as Kraunk had
described it: Beating inside his heart was the big dream
of becoming a butterfly. Somehow he knew that the
dream for more had always been there, he just hadn't
looked long enough. But he was looking now and it was
amazing!

❧

Ernie rushed off to his leaf reporting job to tell Steve all
about his new dream. But Steve's reaction was nothing

like Ernie expected. Instead of being excited for him, ordinary Steve did something very out of the ordinary.

After Ernie described his dream, Steve began to yell at the top of his lungs, "You do not have a dream! You can't have a dream! You're just a caterpillar, and if you have a dream it means that you'll have to leave the island and you will die!"

Ernie didn't know what to say, but he didn't even have a chance, because Steve started shouting and wailing even louder, "You don't have a dream! You don't have a dream! NO, NO, NO!" as though the dream would go away if he shouted loud enough.

Finally Steve, who wasn't used to a lot of physical activity, got tired of yelling and was quiet. Ernie stayed silent for another moment, just to be sure his friend wasn't going to start up again, and then asked, "What on earth do you mean, if I have a dream I have to leave the island? Why can't I just stay here and become a butterfly? This is the best thing that has ever happened to me, Steve! I knew there was something missing. I just knew it!"

Steve could take it no longer and in a very upset tone of voice reminded Ernie about the law of the Big Tree: No caterpillar was allowed to become a butterfly unless he or she left the island. No one really knew why the law existed. Perhaps it was because becoming a butterfly was unpredictable and caterpillars were supposed to be predictable. But regardless of the reason, it was the law.

Then looking away from Ernie, Steve quietly told him that he, too, had once dreamed of becoming a butterfly, but decided it was too risky. He told Ernie to do what they had been taught in ordinary bug school. "Just ignore the dream like we used to ignore our curiosity. It goes away after a while." And with that, the plump caterpillar turned and crawled away as gracefully as he could, leaving Ernie alone with a broken dream.

I wish I could say that Ernie didn't take Steve's advice, but he did. He tried to ignore the dream. He made every effort to kill it, suffocate it, and forget about it—anything but dream it. Nothing seemed to work, though. So when Ernie finally tired of trying to get rid of it, he thought maybe he should just try following it. In that moment, it was almost as if his heart sighed with contentment. Things had never felt so right.

That day Ernie quit his ordinary job at the leaf reporting factory. He had told only his parents and Steve about his decision to leave, but because nothing out of the ordinary ever happened at the Big Tree, the whole island soon found out and came to tell him their opinions. None of which were positive, of course.

His father was among those who didn't care for Ernie's new way of thinking. He said, "Son, I just don't think you're ready for something like this, and I don't think it's a good idea at all. You weren't made to do big things. It's that simple."

Ernie's old teacher Gertrude came next. She stood directly in front of him and said, "What kind of example are you setting for my students? Didn't you listen when we warned you about the risks and dangers? We don't do things like this, Ernie. We just don't!"

Harry, an old schoolmate, gave Ernie an intimidating stare and told him, "You're going to fail. You always failed in things like this. Just don't expect me to feel sorry for you."

It seemed to Ernie that every single ordinary bug had come out to give him a different reason not to leave the island. And honestly, they were all pretty good reasons.

Ernie didn't say anything at all; he just listened. By the time everyone had talked to Ernie, he had almost decided to never ever dream again and to give up forever on becoming a butterfly. It just didn't seem worth it. And when he thought about it, the idea of becoming a butterfly was pretty intimidating. It was such a *big* dream.

Suddenly, the crowd parted as a familiar figure slowly made his way through. It was Kraunk. I wish I could say that the crowd's parting was a show of respect, but the truth was, the ordinary bugs feared him and backing up was just a normal reaction.

Kraunk sat down next to Ernie and in a quiet voice told him, "I know that every one of these ordinary bugs has given you a reason not to pursue your dream. Their reasons may seem logical, and your dream probably seems impossible and unreachable. But if you forsake this dream, you will forsake the life you *know* you were meant to live. I know you're afraid. Being comfortable, though, isn't worth it if it means that you have to die inside. Fear is real, yes. But so is the dream. If you don't listen to your heart and follow the dream, you'll always wonder about what could have happened. The only way you will surely fail is if you don't ever try."

And with that, Kraunk made his way back through the silent crowd and headed home.

Ernie let Kraunk's words sink in for a few moments while hundreds of beady bug eyes rested on him. He decided that Kraunk was right—it wasn't worth giving up his dream just because he was afraid. And so he shouted, "Good-bye!" and turned his back on the stunned crowd. He found a small piece of driftwood on the beach and climbed aboard. When the tide came in, he let it slowly carry him away from the island and toward the unknown.

A few hours later Ernie reached the shore of a new, very unordinary-looking place. He was scared and extremely uncomfortable, but right beside that discomfort was his dream and it was beating so much louder now. He was here to become a butterfly. He was here to fly! Could this really be happening?

Ernie walked around until he came upon what looked like a condominium of cocoons. Excitedly he tried to talk to the caterpillars inside the cocoons, but they wouldn't reply. He thought this odd, but then spotted a bug sitting at a desk in front of a nearby tree. "You looking to rent some cocoon space, young bug?" asked the clerk. Ernie never expected to have to pay someone in order to become a butterfly. He figured it was just supposed to happen naturally. The bug at the desk informed him that not only did he have to pay, but the metamorphosis would also require that he remain in the cocoon for months. And even then he would have to go to a whole new place in order to get his wings.

Ernie had never heard about this before. Of course, because no one at home ever spoke of becoming a butterfly he had not known what to expect—but this definitely wasn't it. Ernie was so disappointed that he began to think about going back home to his small island. At least there he always knew what to expect. The Big Tree was reliable, and it wasn't scary because they all knew their place and always did things that were familiar.

But then he remembered Kraunk's words: "If you don't listen to your heart and follow the dream, you'll always wonder about what could have happened." Ernie had hoped it would be easier, but he also knew this dream was worth fighting for. And that was exactly what he determined to do.

Ernie got a job doing something he had never done before and began saving up enough money to rent the cocoon space. The job didn't pay much, though, and as the days and weeks passed, Ernie's frustration began to grow. Every morning he thought about giving up, and every night he went to sleep discouraged that he was still a fat caterpillar with a dream. But he kept going until one day he had finally earned enough to rent the space.

It wasn't an easy task squeezing himself into a small cocoon. It seems that caterpillars in these parts didn't eat quite as much as they did back home. But he finally got in, and the waiting began.

Months went by and seasons changed, while inside the cocoon changes were also happening. Then one spring day, Ernie's cocoon began to break apart.

It broke slowly at first, but Ernie quickly became more and more impatient, shaking the whole branch as he fought to free himself from the cocoon. Ernie was more ready than anything to see if it had really worked.

And it had!

The cocoon broke open wide to reveal that the fat caterpillar had been transformed into a butterfly— without wings yet, of course. Still, Ernie could almost feel himself flying. But something inside of him had changed, too. All the frustration from the waiting and working had been washed away. His dream beat louder than ever, and so he immediately set out for the land where his wings waited for him.

Ernie found that although he couldn't fly, already his steps were lighter.

A few hours later, Ernie arrived at the gate of the land that the bug behind the desk had described to him. The gate towered high over him and was guarded by giant ants. Ernie became scared again as he looked down and realized that he was a lot smaller than he used to be. But he just *had* to get his wings. He couldn't give up now!

Ernie mustered up all the courage he had and said in a loud voice, "Excuse me, but I'm here to get my wings." Several of the ants turned and stared at him.

"Uh... I mean, to get my wings, please," Ernie said.

The ants busted out in laughter at this outspoken butterfly. One of the soldier ants told Ernie there was no way he was getting his wings unless he fought the ant and won. Ernie was outnumbered, outweighed, out-everythinged!

"Okay," Ernie said. "I'll fight you."

The laughter immediately died away, and the soldier ant glared down at him. Ernie tried to look as though he wasn't afraid, but he knew he wasn't doing a very good job of it.

"You know what, little butterfly? Normally, I would fight you. But I'm pretty impressed at your courage so I'm going to let you have your wings without a fight."

And with that, the ant tossed Ernie a new pair of wings.

Ernie didn't know what to say. He had heard about these ants and knew that they never gave up a pair of wings without a fight. Maybe, just maybe, someone was looking out for him. Ernie stared down at the wings and then back up at the ant. And then he looked back at the wings.

"You'd better get out of here before I change my mind, little butterfly!"

Ernie realized that he hadn't moved and quickly said a quiet "Thanks" before he turned and walked away from the gate with a pair of wings in his hands—something he never imagined he would be holding. Something everyone told him he would never be able to get. But he had. He really had.

Ernie gently put the wings on his back, and he smiled as he realized that this was what he had been made for. This was a life he wasn't supposed to wonder about—this was the life he was supposed to live! And with that, Ernie's wings lifted him into the air.

The funny thing is, Ernie realized, his heart had started flying before his feet had left the ground.

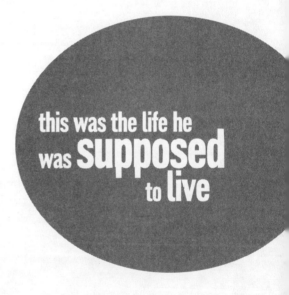

this was the life he was **supposed** to live

One of the biggest **problems** we confront in **pursuing our dream** is simply being able to find it

dreams:
the reason we're here

Have you ever wondered why life holds moments when
your heart beats faster than normal? Or wondered what is
it about our dreams that stir and inspire us so much?
What is it about a dreamless life that is so unappealing? I
wish it weren't true, but life quickly falls from dream-
dominated to dream-forsaken. Every day we grow up, we
let go of those childhood dreams, which is natural in most
ways. But instead of replacing them with different dreams
that don't involve fairy tales, we replace them with the
boring routine of life. We take our dreams and bury them
underneath our disappointments and expect them to die.
We disconnect ourselves from that part of our heart and
live off the rest of it.

And for a while that tactic works. But think for a

moment about those childhood dreams of saving the world and making it better. When those dreams are gone, all the focus on using your talents to help others (no matter how unrealistic) seems to have nowhere else to go but on ourselves. Could it be that killing our dreams kills a part of us that was meant to give us direction and show us our place in this world? Could it be that killing our dreams takes us out of the picture we were meant to be in and places us all alone? Perhaps that's why dreams can't and don't die. Just as almost anything can happen to the lead character in an action movie without killing him, the most important part of who you are doesn't die, either...no matter how many bullets are shot at it.

If you were to stop for a few moments right now and just listen to your heart, what do you think it would tell you? If you could quiet all the distractions you've used to drown out your heart, what dream do you think it might whisper to you? Is it telling you about sports, career, ministry, people, a certain person, a way of life? Is it asking you why you never chased old dreams it spoke to you about, or why you aren't chasing the new dreams found there now? Is it possible that the God of the universe has given you this dream now to communicate His plans for you? Could it be that your dream is meant to be followed and not forgotten?

One of the biggest problems we confront in pursuing our dream is simply being able to *find* it. I was six years old when I first became convinced that God was having trouble communicating with me, so I decided to help him out a little bit. I set up a glass full of water on my tiny square plastic table. For some reason I thought that the harder you squeezed your eyes shut, the more God would listen. So I would turn my back on the little table, squeeze my eyes shut, and pray, "Dear God, if your answer is yes, then *please,* PLEASE (eyes squeezed really hard here!) let the glass be empty when I turn back around." Needless to say, a full glass always stared back at me when I turned around.

This went on for quite a while until I came up with a brilliant idea to make sure God understood that the glass was supposed to be *empty* if the answer was yes. So I asked Him a question to which I was certain the answer was yes. The question was probably something spiritually mature and meaningful like "Are there four Teenage Mutant Ninja Turtles?" Regardless, I still turned around to find that the glass was full.

Many years have gone by since I allowed the amount of water in a glass to make my decisions in life, and I have since learned that God doesn't need us to invent ways to help Him communicate with us, though it would be nice if we had tangible signs to help us find our dream. Something like "Your Dream, Next Three Exits."

Unfortunately, too many of us believe that a life lived following our deepest dreams is a life wasted. Or at least an impossibility for most of us. Sure, we've heard of people who are "living the dream." But we figure that these people must be totally different. They're special. Maybe members of some kind of Magic Dreamers Association that someone forgot to mention to us.

We forget that these people live and move and breathe—just like we do! The only difference is that they chose to listen to the whisper of the dream and pursue it with everything they had. The rest of us have chosen to ignore our dreams, to abandon them along the paths of life. And so we lose the essence of who we were meant to become. We lose the incredible wonder of living for something greater than ourselves.

Dream Testing

Every heart has a dream. It doesn't matter what kind of person you are. *Every* heart has a dream. Even yours.

When God formed your heart and shaped your strengths and passions, He took a look at the big plan we call His Divine Will, which is really His Dream. God then took a part of His Dream—let's say from point A to point B—and placed it in your heart as a small seed that would grow over your lifetime. Your talents, abilities, and passions are all related to that dream. Of course, your dream is just a tiny part of His Dream, but no one can do it quite like you can. And no one will get as much fulfillment in doing it as you will.

But how do you find your dream?

How do you know your dream when you see it?

One of the first things you need to do is to listen to your heart. After all, that's where God has placed the dream He has for you. But there are other clues, too. Not only does your heart whisper to you, but every characteristic, every talent, every trait you have leaves footprints and fingerprints—all directing you to the center of your dream.

Take a moment and wander down each of these paths leading to your dream. If you want to see your dream getting clearer by the moment, grab a pen and write down your thoughts about these Five Dream Clarifiers:

1. *The Test of Your Heartbeat.* What is it that makes you truly come alive? What excites you like nothing else? This is the thing that, when you think of doing it, makes everything fall by the wayside in comparison. When you think about doing this thing, your heart beats faster and your emotions rise up, saying, "Go for it!"

2. *The Test of Your Talents.* What are you naturally good at—and find easy to do? What talents do

you have that other people recognize and encourage? Never look for your dream where your weaknesses lie. Dreams lie in the realm of your greatest areas of gifting.

3. *The Test of Your Daydreams.* What type of things do you daydream about in math class when your teacher has created a new level of boring and all you're hearing are the trombone-droning words of the teacher in the Charlie Brown cartoons, "Wah wah, wah wah wah"? How would you finish this sentence: "If only I could…"?

4. *The Test of Your Heroes.* Who are your heroes? Who are the people you look up to? And what kinds of dreams have they reached? Don't just look at the superstars, but look at those people about whom you find yourself saying, "I would love to do what they do."

5. *The Test of Guaranteed Success.* If you had all the money you could ever want and were guaranteed that you would be successful at anything, what would you choose to do? I mean, *after* you made a million dollars, had your own superband, were the world's top soccer scorer, and were happily married to the person of your dreams and living in the house of your dreams!

Although some of these questions may seem as irrelevant as the mineral content of the soil in India, your answers will reveal not only more about the person you are, but also the direction you must travel to find and fulfill your dream.

But before we go any further, let's take a look at the Person who created your dream. We'll call Him the Dream Giver. He's the one who placed that dream within your heart in the first place—and then handcrafted you to be the only person who could perfectly achieve that dream. Not only is His Dream for you amazing and intricately shaped, but so are you! In all His wisdom and kindness, the Dream Giver dreamt up the perfect dream and then created the perfect dreamer—you.

If you don't view Him correctly, you will never truly understand your dream. Unfortunately, many people think of God as a harsh principal who stalks you until you mess up and then, as a punishment, He forces you to work at something you *hate* doing. For a while, I thought of God that way.

But God doesn't want us to find that one thing we despise doing and then do it to show our obedience to Him. If He did, the world would be populated by nothing but halfhearted, miserable people doing things they hate and aren't good at. Everyone would wake up on the wrong side of the bed every day. In fact, there wouldn't be a "right" side of the bed at all! Life would be like the *Jerry*

Springer Show, where everyone is in a bad mood and mad at everyone else for no particular reason.

Just think about the backward logic of this way of thinking. If God forced people to do things they hated and weren't good at, how much of His Dream do you think would be achieved on this earth? But if God invited people to do the things they love to do—and are good at doing—how much more of His Dream could be fulfilled?

God created our hearts to desire what He wants us to do, and you can see it in the youngest of children. Ask any surgeon if he practiced doctoring when he was little. Ask any famous singer if she spent hours practicing in the mirror with a hairbrush for a microphone. How could a person who passes out at the sight of blood ever make a good doctor? Or how could a person who's scared of heights ever make a good skydiving instructor, or a short, clumsy boy make a good NBA player? They wouldn't. (But if they did become those things, everyone would be afraid to go to doctors or jump out of planes, and NBA basketball would be a most frustrating sport to watch!)

In the same way, God didn't create you to despise doing something you are good at and are meant to do. He didn't create you to *hate* your dream. That wouldn't be a dream, but a nightmare.

What Is a Dream?

So what exactly is a dream? How will you know when you've found the right dream? Let's look at a few characteristics of every dream—many that will surprise you.

Characteristic 1: The Impossibility of the Dream

Every dream feels impossible. You don't know how you could ever achieve the dream. A million "But I can't…" thoughts flood your mind. Who are you, anyway, to think you could achieve this dream? You haven't had an experience even remotely like this dream. So if you feel as though you just can't do it, you may be on the right road to the dream!

Characteristic 2: The Size of the Dream

Every dream seems too huge, too big, too overwhelming. You look at your minimal resources and the massive size of the dream and you start to feel hopeless. How can you ever achieve such a big thing? It may surprise you, but the Dream Giver never gives anyone a small or even medium-sized dream. He wants you to trust Him and go for it in faith. So if you feel as though the job's too big for you, you may be on the right road to the dream!

Characteristic 3: The Future Tense of the Dream

Your dream is a picture of something that hasn't yet come true. The dream lives in the future and beckons you to move beyond the present to achieve it. Dreams initially dwell in your imagination and ask you to make them into reality. So if you feel as though your dream is only a fantasy, you may be on the right road to the dream!

Characteristic 4: The Heart of the Dream

Every dream is a picture of something coming true—something that someone wishes could come true. Ultimately, the dream is the fulfillment of someone's need and desire. Dreams may start with our own wishes, but they seek to grow beyond ourselves into the fulfillment of someone else's needs and wishes as well. So if you feel as though your dream is not only for yourself but also for someone else, you may be on the right road to the dream!

Your Dream Is Waiting

Finding your dream will most likely lead to the initial feeling of overwhelming joy. But accompanying the discovery of every dream are also feelings of shock and fear. After all, your dream is straight from the heart of God, and He dreams BIG dreams. Sadly, at the first sensing of fear many people turn and walk away from their dream, believing that their fear is a sign that the dream is not from God. What a tragic misconception! Fear is many times only a clear sign that you need the hand of God upon you in order to do your dream. It's a challenge—one you will long to do despite any fear.

If you've ever tried to blow out some of those magic relighting candles, then you know how it feels to discover your dream. Dreams will not and cannot be blown out. In fact, dreams can't be ignored. They surface time after time throughout the day, trying desperately to get us to pay attention to them.

Anything that remotely resembles our dream awakens our heart, and we become like little children when they meet Santa Claus for the first time. There's a longing to know more, but at the same time we've heard the rumors that he's not real—so we aren't sure if we want to get to know him or just hang back for a while. But unlike Santa, dreams are very real and play a bigger role in our lives than an imaginary person who steals our cookies one day out of the year when we're young.

Some people try to ignore their dream by drowning it out with everyday distractions,

Your dream shapes who you are

hoping that the uncomfortable feeling will go away soon. It's a little like the feeling you get when you have that dream of going to school in your underwear—all you want to do is wake up and have things go back to normal!

Then there are those people who will do anything to distance themselves from the dream, to make it seem impersonal and impossible and, therefore, not worth thinking about.

What most people don't realize is that their dream is at the root of much of what they choose to do in life. The dream determines many of your daily actions without your even being aware. You may already be pursuing your dream without even realizing that the dream beats loudly in your heart. Your dream shapes who you are; you don't shape your dream!

Perhaps you haven't quite figured out your dream and you're wondering if it's supposed to mean something that you wanted to be an astronaut when you were a kid. In the coming chapters, you'll learn more about identifying and clarifying your dream so you'll know exactly what it is you're chasing.

So begin thinking about those questions listed earlier and about talents, passions, and childhood dreams and see what kind of picture starts coming together. Don't worry if the picture remains a bit fuzzy and unclear. We're just getting started!

We're **just** getting
started

Fear is the **enemy,**
and it's at constant war with your
dream

your comfort zone:
life-size huggies

Spend more than five minutes with most little kids and you'll probably hear the word *mine* at least a dozen times. Everything is "mine." Even *your* things are mine! And it's amazing how long and hard some kids will fight for whatever they consider mine—even if the object didn't mean a thing to them five minutes ago. Nothing is held back and the tears are real.

I sometimes wonder what happened to that fighter inside us. Why is it that we are so quick to stop listening to our dreams? Have we forgotten how to be passionate about what is "mine"?

Don't get me wrong. I'm not suggesting that we revert to the selfish and childish behavior of toddlers and fight over Barbie dolls and toy cars. But I do wish we would fight a little harder for our dreams.

The fact is, we *don't* fight for our dreams simply because they threaten our feelings of comfort and security.

What comes to mind when you think of comfort? Perhaps you think about the warm bed you reluctantly crawl out of every morning.

Most of us don't think of comfort as a primary reason we do the things we do. But let's look at TV commercials for a second. Their job is to sell you stuff and lots of it. And they do it well. TV commercials always talk about the most comfortable and convenient shoes, clothing, car, insurance, grocery store, Internet service—the most comfortable *everything*.

But what if I told you that your need for comfort is one of the biggest threats to your dream? What if I told you that most people *never* follow their dream because it exists outside their comfort zone?

To get a visual image of your comfort zone, picture four high walls arranged around your life. Inside you feel secure, safe, able, and unchallenged. Everything you can do, and are comfortable doing, lies within these four walls. It's like a gigantic Huggies diaper wrapped around your life. As long as you do everything *inside* the diaper, it's all good. (I'm pretty sure that's their point, anyway.)

Now take a few steps toward the open window, where the unknown awaits just outside in the darkness. Suddenly you don't feel quite so comfortable anymore. You find yourself feeling challenged, insecure, threatened, and all-around scared to death. Not at all appealing! So what do you do? You quickly run back to the middle of your comfort zone and jump into the pile of pillows waiting for you there. Fear cannot reach you in this place, and you sigh as a feeling of security starts to return.

It doesn't take too many times of walking near the edge of your comfort zone before you realize that feelings of fear arise whenever you begin to walk away from what you know how to do and are used to doing. But remember, all those inhibitions and fears are internal. *You* decide how big your comfort zone is and how much you will let it control you.

Back when my dad was a college professor, he decided to teach his students a little lesson about comfort zones. On a day when they were scheduled to give oral presentations, my dad placed a piece of black tape between the classroom door and the podium. The students had to cross over the black tape in order to get to their seats, but most didn't even notice it there. At the beginning of class, before the speeches began, my dad told the students that before their speech was over, they had to walk out to the piece of black tape and stand on it for a few seconds while giving their presentation.

Suddenly, that piece of black tape became the most intimidating thing in the world. The students were terrified of walking out from behind the safety of the podium and standing on the black tape in the middle of the room. It felt unnatural, stupid, and certainly outside their comfort zone. And yet when entering the room, every single student had crossed over that piece of tape without any feelings of fear and inhibition. It wasn't the tape that scared them; it was the boundaries of their comfort zone that were being threatened and stretched by a piece of tape.

Fear Is the Enemy

So why step out of our comfort zone? Why would we *ever* want to make ourselves feel uncomfortable? It just seems illogical and torturous, right? After all, the world encourages us to "do what feels good," and feeling insecure definitely does *not* feel good.

> One of the greatest **tragedies** in life occurs when we begin to forget the very **reason** we're alive

There's only one problem with staying in your comfort zone.

Your dream isn't inside it.

Every single dream, hope, and aspiration you will ever have is located outside those four walls and that Huggies diaper. Small dreams are waiting right outside those walls, while big dreams are a bit further off. But regardless of how big or small the dream is, you're never going to find it inside your comfort zone.

As long as the walls of your comfort zone remain standing, fear will be there. And as long as you remain inside these walls, your dream will remain forever untouched and your heart will never be satisfied. Sounds pretty depressing, huh?

The truth is, there's no way to completely destroy fear.

But the awesome part is that there is a way to reach your dream despite it.

You see, each morning we awake inside the same comfort zone where we fell asleep. And each morning fear comes knocking and asks our permission to control us for that day. And almost always our subconscious answer to fear's question is, *Why yes, of course you can control me today.*

We allow fear to hold us back from our dream on a daily basis. We allow fear to determine what we say and do. We pretty much allow fear to define our life for us. Fear stands at the door of our heart and guards our dream within, never allowing us in—or our dream out. And after fear stands there long enough, we forget what our dream even looks like. One of the greatest tragedies in life occurs when we begin to forget the *very reason we're alive.*

Fear is the enemy, and it's at constant war with your dream. Fear wants to consume you, but so does your dream. You can either be controlled by the hand of fear, or you can be consumed by your dream in the presence of fear. Fear doesn't leave, even when you are consumed by your dream—but it does lose its power to control you.

Unfortunately, the world we live in encourages people to remain within their comfort zones, unable even to *talk* about being afraid. Too many churches are inhibited in their worship and would probably look down on King David's undignified public dancing to the Lord (see 2 Samuel 6:16). Society teaches us to hide our true emotions and pretend to be someone we're not.

We are told to stay back from potentially dangerous situations and leave them to experienced professionals. The world is so willing to help each of us fashion a cage that keeps us in our place. Don't get me wrong—I don't think it's a good idea to play cops and robbers in the inner city. But I do think this constant emphasis toward playing it safe, especially when it comes to our dream, can be more damaging than we realize.

A few nights ago I came across a movie while flipping through the channels. In the scene I watched, thirteen businessmen were sitting in a circle. I immediately figured out that the woman in the circle was a psychiatrist when she said, "Tell me how you feel about that." (I have no idea why, with all the money they make, psychiatrists

haven't been able to come up with something new to say.)
Anyway, all thirteen of the businessmen believed that they
were inhabited by the spirit of a lake monster who was
crying out for help because of pollution in the lake. After
a few moments of quiet discussion, one man finally broke
down and admitted that he was *afraid*. Soon the room was
filled with lively conversation as they all admitted to
having similar feelings of fear.

Don't worry, I'm not trying to compare your fear with
the kind you find in a grade-Z horror flick. My point is
that, although it is rarely talked about, *everyone* experiences
fear when stepping out of their comfort zone. It would be
awesome if everyone would admit when they're afraid,
but a lot of people simply refuse to accept that they are
human and instead try to act like Johnny Bravo. Maybe
they think their accomplishments won't seem as great if
people know they are only acting out of fear.

But I promise you, you aren't the only one afraid of
the unknown.

Breaking Through Is Hard to Do

One of the biggest and most controlling misconceptions
about comfort zones is that they need to be overcome
only once. *You can never break your comfort zone.* Even if you
went at it with a sledgehammer, a machete, and a few
black belt kung fu moves, you still couldn't break through
for good.

But what you *can* do is push the borders of your comfort zone out farther, making room for more things you are comfortable doing and, therefore, *fewer things you are fearful of doing.* It does take time before you are truly comfortable doing some new things. For example, you may have to speak in front of the class a few times before your fear of public speaking grows weaker—but it will grow weaker!

It's easy to look at people who have accomplished amazing dreams and completely overlook the process it took them to get there. We see where they are now and it looks great. But what we can't see are all the times these dreamers walked to the edge of their comfort zones and pushed those walls outward.

I have often wished that somehow I could grow wings and just fly over my walls and land where my dream is. But then I remembered something about the heart of the God we serve: He's concerned not only about our destination, but also every step, stumble, fall, and struggle we experience in getting there. Each time we push back the walls of our comfort zone and take another step toward our dream, we grow a little in our faith while the strength of our fear dies a little.

Granted, it's a long and determined process, but the feeling of standing on that piece of ground you just discovered when you moved the wall of your comfort zone is one of the most awesome feelings *ever* (after you get over that initial scared-to-death feeling). And it's *meant* to be awesome, because it means one more step toward the completion of your dream, and your heart begins to sing just a little louder.

I remember one time when the walls of my comfort zone were shaken. I felt like a cat caught in a washing machine, frantically trying to get out. And yet I didn't want to move, either. It happened on an overcast day in Ireland. The missions team I was with had taken a bus into a small town where we were to spend a few hours getting to know the people there before boarding a ferry. We split into groups of two and started walking around the town. My partner and I talked with a few people, and then we both realized we were meant to go our separate ways for a while—he in one direction and I in another. I started walking through a park, silently praying that God would lead me to the person who was crying out for Him the loudest. When I looked up, I saw the biggest-muscled man I've ever seen in my life. Mr. T would have been intimidated! This guy's arm was as big around as my waist, and the expression on his face was not inviting in the least.

Immediately, the internal struggle of flesh and spirit began—my dream and my comfort zone collided and only one could win. I tried to tell God that this was an unreasonable assignment and that I was all alone. God said, "Trust Me." He reminded me that He isn't bound by logic and reason. I couldn't argue there! I'm sure Joshua felt the same way as he walked around the walls of Jericho blowing horns.

I hesitated a few moments and found myself frustrated at how weak my faith in my God was. Was I going to allow myself to be held captive by my walls of fear and forsake God's calling?

I worked up all the courage I had and walked over to where Muscle Guy was sitting and began to talk to him. In all honesty, I can't remember what words were said, but I do remember seeing the faithfulness of God. As soon as we began talking, God spoke to my heart and said, *Now I want you to see what I see.* Instead of seeing a big, unapproachable man, I saw a hurting soul longing to be held in the arms of God. I saw pain, confusion, and a hunger for his Creator. Within a half hour the guy was thanking me for introducing him to my God (who was now *his* God as well) while tears of joy and freedom ran down his face.

I smiled as I walked away. I realized that my need to feel comfortable was definitely not worth missing out on that encounter.

I wish I could say that I willingly pursue every God-given opportunity that's outside my comfort zone. Many times I haven't. It's so easy to decide that you won't be ruled by the feeling of comfort and security, but it's a whole new thing to start living it out.

Remember, though, that your comfort zone can hold

you back only if you let it. Only *you* can determine how strong the walls of your comfort zone are, and you *always* have enough strength to move them.

I should probably clear up the point that it is natural and healthy to have a comfort zone. Everyone has one. Everyone. Your parents, your friends, movie stars, the man inside the Barney costume. But it's how you deal with your comfort zone that determines how close to your dream you come. Those walls are not meant to stand unmoved.

When you decide to actively push back your comfort zone, expect the evil one to resist you. To fight most effectively, you need to be aware of your opponent's tactics and what resources you need in order to win. You wouldn't challenge a sumo wrestler with a pellet gun, right? But if you were after a crazed squirrel, a pellet gun would be the perfect weapon. You need to approach the task of pushing back your comfort zone with the correct weapons, which means you need to first be aware of how Satan will try and keep you in. And believe me, he will.

In the book of Exodus, God gave Moses this amazing dream to set His people free, and Moses found himself scared out of his mind! He said to God, "O Lord, I have never been eloquent, neither in the past nor since you have spoken to your servant. I am slow of speech and tongue." Moses felt inadequate and unable—feelings most of us have when God asks us to do something out of the ordinary or we set out to do the unimaginable. We feel like the smallest person on earth. But God immediately reassured Moses that He would be with him every step of the way and that he need not be afraid.

Yes, God may ask you to do something that you feel completely incapable of doing, but He will never leave you by yourself. He will never ask something of you that is impossible for Him, though it may seem impossible for you.

Abandoning your dream may seem much more comfortable and less risky than stepping out of your comfort zone. But think what Moses would have missed out on if he had said no to God and stayed within his comfort zone. The Israelites would have remained in captivity without a leader, and they wouldn't have seen God's hand part a sea for them or provide water out of a rock. Who knows, Moses may not even have been in the Bible had he stayed in his comfort zone.

When you make comfort a greater priority than your dream, you stop chasing the dream you were meant to live for. Your dream still cries that soulful tune from a far-off land, but you say no to it, and ultimately no to God. I know it feels scary, but you will never be alone. And those dreams are too amazing not to risk some comfort for.

So keep dreaming and keep reading. There's so much more!

There's so much
more

Border bullies **aren't** who
you **expect** them to be

border bullies:
the playground swing-set kings

The term *border bully* has always reminded me of the big fat kid who would never let anyone swing on the swing set during recess when I was in kindergarten. He never had a good reason why he didn't want anyone on the swings, but he was big and intimidating and most kids decided swinging really wasn't more important than living. But truth be known, a border bully is nothing like this kid, and a border bully can keep you from a lot more than just a swing.

When Comfort Zones Are Shaken

The very outer part of your comfort zone is called BorderLand. It's that part where you have stretched your comfort zone, and your increased comfort zone space begins to shake other people's comfort zones. All the people you come into contact with, such as friends at school, family, and friends at church, overlap your comfort zone. When either their comfort zone or your comfort zone expands, it can create conflict. For example, if your mom decided to transfer to a larger company in another state, your whole family's comfort zone would be rocked, not just hers. If someone's comfort zone shrinks, that also has an effect on others. If a running back for the Packers leaves training camp because he no longer has a passion for football and decides to shrink his comfort zone, all of the players on that team would be affected. The bigger the person's dream and the closer that person is to you, the more your comfort zone will be shaken.

Our natural reaction to someone shaking our comfort zone is to do what we can to stop it. It's hard enough to shake our own comfort zone, but it's even harder when someone else makes it shake and we aren't controlling it. It may not necessarily be that we don't like the other person's dream; it's just that it's affecting us and shaking us up and we want to calm things back down again. So the definition of a border bully is *someone whose comfort zone is affected by a dream that is not their own, and who seeks to stop the dream from continuing any further.*

Recognizing Border Bullies

Have you ever heard any of these phrases?

"What are you possibly thinking?"

"You aren't good enough for that."

"What about all the mistakes you've made before this?"

"You actually expect that to work?"

"You've got to be crazy!"

Chances are you've met a border bully already.

Border bullies usually tell us that our plan is unreasonable, risky, impossible, and that we'll never be able to do it. I'm not talking about how your mom says you're crazy when you tell her that you plan to bungee jump off the interstate bridge. I'm talking about when someone stands at the edge of your comfort zone so you can't walk out any farther and make it shake anymore. Border bullies attack your dream, whether they just stand in your way, try to talk you out of your dream, or aggressively push you back.

But the hardest thing about border bullies is that they usually aren't who you expect them to be. Though border bullies can and may be enemies, they most often are people we love and look up to. When most teenagers are asked who their number one border bullies are, they immediately say their parents. Perhaps your parents don't like the idea of your going to your dream college in another state. Or maybe they point to your weaknesses or

remind you over and over again of your past mistakes and
how your dream can never be reached because of those
very weaknesses. That's discouragement enough to get
anyone to stand still!

The motivation of border bullies isn't necessarily to
attack you or your dream. A lot of times they resist your
dream because *they* feel threatened. They fear losing
something important—their way of life, perhaps, or
maybe even losing you.

One of the most common border bullies is the
alarmist. This bully exclaims, "It's not safe!" He usually
exaggerates the risks because he's afraid for you, or afraid
of how much your dream could affect him.

Another border bully tactic is delay: "Why don't you
wait until you're older?" This border bully seeks to
postpone your dream in hopes that "later" never comes.
He resists change and improvement by making you feel
unable.

One of the hardest things when walking in
BorderLand is to encounter border bullies who you
thought would support you and your dream. Suddenly the
mom who always believed in you has only words of
caution and fear for you. Your dad suddenly remembers
all your past mistakes and tells you that maybe you should
wait until you're more mature. Your friends tell you that
though it's a nice idea, maybe your head is a little too far
in the clouds. Your coach keeps telling you to practice but

doesn't believe you have the skill needed to make the varsity team this year. Your music instructor seems to notice only your mistakes, and by the time the lesson is over, you're sure you are the worst percussionist in the entire world.

One of the first border bullies I can remember was a person I looked up to. Every time I would tell her about my dreams or about the deep things God was teaching me, she would bring up my age and tell me I should just enjoy being young for a while: "You can get to all of that when you're older, but you're only young once!" Though she was right about being young only once, she continually sapped the passion and urgency from my dreams without me even realizing it. My fight for those dreams became weaker and pretty soon I was telling myself, *I'll get to those things when I'm older*—things God wanted done *now!*

Responding to Border Bullies

Now that we know what a border bully says and does, what should we do when one appears? Should we ignore their warnings about risk and weaknesses? Should you wait to fulfill your dream until they're willing to support you? You probably don't think any good can come from your encounters with border bullies, but amazingly enough, good can come from them.

One of the main differences between your comfort

zone and BorderLand is that in your comfort zone you dealt with your insecurity through self-talk. Now, suddenly, other people are making you question whether you are cut out for your dream. Instead of helping you out, they stop you where you are and say things that can't be ignored. And maybe they shouldn't be ignored. We shouldn't just drown out the comments border bullies make. Some things they say or do really can help us.

I remember the first time I punched someone. I was about eight years old and was probably dressed in some ridiculously frilly pink dress. We were visiting my grandparents in Pennsylvania, and we went to their church for the morning. After Sunday school class was over, I was walking down the hall and some boy came over beside me and tried to kiss me. My mom had taught me to be nice to everyone, but I must have completely forgotten that it was Sunday, and so I hit him. Not hard, but hard enough that he stopped trying to kiss me and silently walked away, dazed and deciding that this was not his lucky day. At the age of eight, and in pink frills, I became someone's border bully.

We've all been a border bully to someone at one time or another, whether it was just cautioning them or really pushing them back. So listening when border bullies talk could be more helpful than you think. Perhaps the border bully says, "I don't know if that's a good idea. I mean, have you thought about how this could affect your family, your education, your (fill in the blank)." Well, maybe you hadn't thought of that yet, but needed to.

Border bullies can help you look at your dream a little more carefully and make sure that you are going at it in the best possible way. They can actually help you clarify your dream a little more (though that's usually not what they're trying to do at all).

It's a lot harder to deal with other people's insecurities about your dream than your own insecurity. Problems always sound bigger when people talk about them. It's kind of like telling a person about a fish you caught. Somehow the fish always gets bigger with each person you tell it to until you've caught this humongous whale in your backyard pond! Each time someone mentions a problem to you about your dream, the problem becomes a whole lot bigger and a little more impossible to overcome.

> Problems always sound **bigger** when people **talk** about them

Now let's look at what to do with this "whale" of a problem people are telling you about. Before entering BorderLand, you will have begun to value your dream over feelings of comfort, and as you journey now through this stage, you'll be faced with the decision of whether you will fear man or God more. After listening to the border bullies, you must decide whether to be swayed by them or to take their concerns into consideration, make any adjustments, and then continue to walk toward your dream. It's a lot harder than it sounds, and those of you who have faced this choice know that. So it's good that border bullies are not the only people present in BorderLand.

Those Who Come Alongside

Two more types of people reside in BorderLand, though they are much less common. They are known as *border buddies* and *border busters.* Border buddies support your dream and encourage you in it. They say things like, "That's a great idea," "I know you can do it," "Keep trying." And border busters actually help you pursue your dream. They aren't on the sideline cheering you on; they're right beside you doing whatever it takes to help you make it. They see that the dream is from God and stand beside you until you accomplish it. Border busters are the most awesome people in the entire dream journey, and they will impact you in ways you'll never forget. They are few, but you'll know when you've met one. They won't let you forsake your dream, and you'll be thankful to them for the rest of your life. They know the song of your heart and can sing it back to you when you've forgotten it. They help you see what you *should* be looking at, but aren't. They are the people helping to make sure that the opinions of others don't matter more to you than they should.

When God told Moses to go to Pharaoh and order
the release of His people, Moses responded, "But suppose
that they will not believe me or listen to my voice;
suppose they say, 'The Lord has not appeared to you.'"
Before Moses has even moved a muscle, he's begun to
anticipate the border bullies at the end of his comfort
zone. And he definitely ran into a few. Even the people he
was trying to set free were border bullies! It can't get
much harder than that. But Moses kept going, and God
blessed his endurance even in the midst of thousands of
border bullies.

Probably none of us will ever face that much
opposition in the pursuit of our dreams, but we all have
our days when it feels like we're all alone. *Maybe if I just give
up,* you think, *they'll leave me alone.* And you know what?
You're right. When you're not moving, there's no reason
for the people around you to try and quiet their comfort
zones, because you're not shaking them. But as soon as
you start moving toward your dream, their quiet lives will
suddenly become not so quiet anymore, and all eyes will
be focused on the one person moving—you.

The biggest misconception—and the biggest way you
can stumble at this stage—is to decide not to move
forward until others are in favor of your dream. I would
love it if everyone was supportive of my dream when I
know it's from God, but that won't happen. Nor should I
look at opposition as an indication that my dream isn't of

God. It's just a chance for my dream to become stronger inside of me.

I wish we lived in a perfect world, but as you know it's far from it. Big kids rule the swing sets in kindergarten, and people can intimidate us when we get older and try to accomplish our dreams. But we can choose not to let others' opinions shape us, and instead live in fear of God and keep heading toward that dream.

One day you'll look back and be glad that you didn't listen to your border bullies. You'll be glad you didn't live your life the way they wanted you to live it. You won't be like the many who find themselves upset at how life turned out, not realizing that they're upset because this isn't the life *they* wanted; it's the life everyone else wanted for them. So keep running toward your God-given dream and encouraging others to reach theirs (unless their dream is to be the first to kiss you at the age of eight!).

Keep going, dreamer, and know that the God of heaven is smiling down on you.

Keep going,
dreamer

WasteLands are not in
vain

wasteland:
broken expectations and sandy deserts

Have you ever developed expectations only to have them completely and in every way destroyed? Perhaps you entered a relationship with a guy/girl only to find that he/she wasn't anything like you had thought. Perhaps you expected something to last forever that continued for only a few months, like a commitment to get good grades or work out a few times a week. Or maybe you had higher expectations for yourself and the way you were going to act in a situation, or standards that you were going to keep, that didn't seem to hold true either.

Expectation vs. Reality

First dating relationships are often good examples of
expectation conflicting with reality. Nearly everyone I have
ever talked to has had unrealistically high expectations for
that first love. Most are convinced they are going to end up
with the first person they fall for. They are convinced that
it's not possible for a love so perfect to end in pain. They
are convinced that the person who seems to match their
hopes and prayers will never disappoint or hurt them. And
sometimes it turns out how both people had hoped, and
they find that "can't let go of, don't want to let go of, and
won't let go of" kind of person in the first one they date.
But it usually isn't like that. Our hearts usually are
disappointed and broken a few times, and expectations
usually change before it turns out how we were almost
certain it was going to that first time.

I'm sure a lot of you can identify with the expectation
of believing someone who says, "I'll be there forever for
you." And they probably meant it, you probably believed
it, but it might not have come true. Maybe your dad said
he'd be there at your game, but he wasn't. Or your mom
said she'd be there for you, but it feels like work is more
important to her than you ever will be and you've stopped
expecting anything at all. We all have expectations, and it
hurts when they're broken. It hurts bad.

So we brace ourselves for life. We brace ourselves to get
hurt, to be disappointed, to be let down. And sometimes

that makes it a little easier and a little less painful.

But when it comes to dreams, most of us don't brace ourselves. For some reason we expect an easy ride. And trust me, pursuing your dream isn't always easy.

You're probably wondering just what this WasteLand stage is. So far we've covered three stages: (1) We've reached deep within our heart and found the dream; (2) we've carried it to the limits of our comfort zone while our knees shook and our hands trembled; and (3) we've broken through the border. By now you probably feel as if you've had just about all you can handle and are ready for that breath of fresh air. But as you shut your eyes and break out of the border, you're met with a sharp wind blowing sand across your face, and within moments you're covered in a thin layer of grit. Broken expectations? Most definitely.

Not long ago I returned from a summer in Peru only to enter straight into a WasteLand. The whole summer had been test after test after test, and emotionally I felt as if I could barely stand. But God had been glorified through the testing, and many comfort zones were broken through and a lot of "self" died that trip. By the end I was praying that God would use me to do more of His will and to realize more of the dream He had placed in my heart. I was expecting to go home and pursue the dream now that I had so much more space in my comfort zone, but what happened was beyond what I ever would have imagined.

I sometimes can anticipate when struggles will come my way and summon the strength to face them, but listening to my dad talk about what had happened while I was in Peru and realizing that he was about to tell me we were moving to Africa, I suddenly didn't feel so strong. (I think it's almost every American Christian's secret prayer not to be sent to Africa. "I'll go anywhere, do anything for you, God, but please don't send me to Africa." Now I'm praying that God would please not send me to Hawaii. I'll let you know if it works!) I can't remember all that was said that day, but I do remember thinking I wasn't ready for more testing. I was ready to do my dream, not move to Africa. Little did I know, this was the next stage toward my dream.

Wings to Fly

When God hands us a dream, our initial reaction is usually, "I could never do this!" And we're right. We never could. It's out of our comfort zone, often unsupported by so many people, and completely unrealistic. It almost feels as if God is asking us to fly. And in some ways He is. But what if He were to give us wings to help us fly? Would asking us to fly be a little different then? Well, WasteLand is where those wings are built and shaped so that when He asks us to fly, we can.

One of the best examples of WasteLand found in the Bible involves David. Here's the scene: he's the youngest of all his brothers and has just been told that he will be king.

I'm sure thoughts of grandeur, wealth, and beautiful women (hey, he's a guy!) filled his head, and he was ready to go lead the people. But that's not quite what happened next.

For the next few years—not months, years—David spent his time shepherding sheep and then hiding out in caves with outlaws, beggars, discontented and distressed people. I'm sure this wasn't making much sense to David. He was probably ready to go do the dream and become king. But through all these seemingly wasted and meaningless years, David was being prepared and taught how to lead effectively by learning how to lead the most difficult people. God was preparing him to become king through situations where David couldn't see the hand of God, but just had to trust that it was there somewhere. And it was.

Preparing to Pursue Your Dream

WasteLand is a huge killer of dreams, mainly because people misunderstand God's motives in the WasteLand. They don't see that He is preparing them to be more capable to fulfill the dream. They think He's seeking to test them until they break and until the dream dies. It's one of the hardest things to trust another person with yourself— even God. To place your heart, life, soul, and dreams into His hands to shape no matter how much it hurts. It feels vulnerable, uncomfortable, unnatural, and in all honesty, it feels unsafe. But those are the moments when you have to trust that God's heart is good and that He will never test you beyond what you can bear (see 1 Corinthians 10:13).

I love the way The Message translates the section in James that talks about testing: "Consider it a sheer gift, friends, when tests and challenges come at you from all sides. You know that under pressure, your faith-life is forced into the open and shows its true colors. *So don't try to get out of anything prematurely.* Let it do its work so you become mature and well-developed, not deficient in any way" (italics mine).

WasteLand is a series of those tests of faith. And trust me, you'll have many moments where you'll want to "get out of things prematurely." We all have them, and the temptation to rebel against God is pretty strong here. But sin or rebellion will get you absolutely nowhere. If you sin or rebel, then you will be disciplined, and discipline is not at all the same as WasteLand. One is the result of doing something wrong; the other is the result of doing something right. Look at the end of the verse. What does it promise as a result of all those tests and challenges? It promises that you will be "mature and well-developed, not deficient in any way" (or in some translations, "not lacking a thing"). The tests are meant to make you more able to pursue your dream—to lessen those feelings of inadequacy and inability that you experienced in the comfort zone.

Just look at the story of Joseph. Here is a man betrayed by his own brothers and sold into slavery. His brothers didn't just use his toothbrush to clean the toilet or pick on him mercilessly; they actually sold him. And all he had done was tell them about a dream God had given him. From there he was sold to a man under Pharaoh named Potiphar. God blessed him there, and Joseph was eventually put in charge of everything within Potiphar's household. But Potiphar's wife had a crush on Joseph, and when she realized that he was going to remain faithful to God and not do what she wanted him to, she betrayed him.

Again, Joseph had done nothing wrong. He actually had done everything right, but he was placed in jail for years. And once again God blessed him, and the warden eventually put him in charge of the prison. Later Joseph deciphered the dreams of two people who had served Pharaoh, and the one who was released from prison completely forgot about Joseph for two more years. It was only when Pharaoh had a dream that needed interpretation that the man released from prison remembered Joseph. God enabled Joseph to interpret the dream, and he was then placed in charge of all Egypt with only Pharaoh above him.

But what a hard WasteLand Joseph had to go through to get there. Betrayal by his family and by the wife of the person he faithfully served. Unjustly placed in prison for years and then forgotten by the person who was supposed to mention him to Pharaoh. I'm sure Joseph woke up some mornings wondering what on earth he could possibly have done to deserve such abuse, and thinking that all this was just a "waste." But then we see the verse, "The Lord was with Joseph." The Bible tells us that the Lord was with Joseph in Potiphar's household when all Joseph did prospered. It tells us that the Lord was with Joseph in prison when he was put in charge of all prisoners and held responsible for everything that happened there. The Lord was with Joseph and preparing him every step of the way in WasteLand.

What do you think Joseph learned when he oversaw Potiphar's entire household? What about when he was placed in charge of the prison? He learned leadership. He learned how to rule, organize, and manage, and with the hand of God upon him he was successful. Do you think he would have been prepared to rule all of Egypt if he hadn't had these experiences first? Joseph would never have been prepared for that task if he hadn't first been sold to Potiphar and placed in prison to learn what he had to in order to fulfill the dream God had set him apart for. There in WasteLand God was teaching and training him so that when the time came for the fulfillment of God's dream for Joseph to rule Egypt, he would be prepared for the position he was placed in. And not only did he rule Egypt, more importantly he provided a refuge for his father and brothers during a time of severe famine, and from that family came the nation of Israel. Though I'm sure that many times Joseph didn't understand what God was up to, he trusted Him. God blessed Joseph and led him to his dream, but only after he passed through WasteLand.

God's Hand in Your WasteLand

WasteLand isn't meaningless wanderings in the desert, but a blind walk closer to the dream. Each step makes us more able to do what God will eventually ask of us. Every WasteLand will bring moments of pain, confusion, ache, loneliness— pretty much everything we like to avoid. But what we learn in WasteLand is not in vain at all. It's preparing us to more effectively pursue our dream.

Every WasteLand will bring moments of pain

I recently met someone who has already become a close friend of mine. It took only moments of talking with him before I knew which stage of his dream he is in. He's originally from South Africa, where I've been living, but is playing cricket and rugby and studying in England away from all the comfort zones and the Christian support he's used to. He told me how he feels as if he's standing with his back against a wall trying with everything inside him to defend God. He told me how his so-called friends there attack his moral standards more than a complete stranger would dare to do. I saw the pain in his eyes as he spoke and knew that he was walking through a long and testing WasteLand that was testing him far more than he ever expected. But what he didn't know then was that the people who knew him well before he left South Africa couldn't stop talking about how much closer to God he had drawn and how much stronger his faith had become. He chose to fight for what he believes and is continuing to do so even now. God is honoring him greatly and is taking that weary wasteland heart and filling it back up. He is giving him the strength to go on and forever changing him—so much so that everyone around him noticed.

WasteLands are not in vain. They are more important than we will ever know.

I have questioned God's will for me quite a few times when the plans my heart desired and longed for broke into pieces that could never be put back together. In those times, I was staring so intently at the broken pieces that I couldn't see God beside me with His own pieces creating an even more beautiful picture than I could have dreamed of. It's not all a waste; it's just that He wants your trust, and if you could see the whole picture, it wouldn't require you to have faith in the unseen. But when you see what He makes with those pieces, you'll know that it was worth it.

So as you continue walking in the WasteLand, know that there's a reason for your wandering and for the tests. And when you're living out your dream and looking back on this time that seemed to be such a waste, you'll see how it all fit together and you'll be so grateful for the preparation.

Don't let yourself give up. He will never let something break if He doesn't have another plan in mind, whether it's to put it back together later and make it stronger than before, or to bring a whole new plan before you that you've never imagined. Either way, it's more than worth it!

Don't let yourself give up

Sanctuary is a **time** when **God** reaches **down** from **heaven**

sanctuary:
mountain climbs and muscular fighters

I remember one of the first times I entered Sanctuary. I was with a group of kids on a small, scarcely populated island, known as the Erin Isle. We had just spent a month doing intense mission work with insane hours and were debriefing for about two days before heading home. During the past week the stomach flu had passed from one team member to the next (I'm sure because of unsanitary dishwashing by guy team members) and we were all still pretty weak. We split up for about four or five hours and spread out over the entire island. I had planned on sitting by the shore and listening to the ocean waves on the sand, but as soon as I sat on the beach, I felt a small tug on my heart telling me to "climb higher."

Emotionally, spiritually, and physically exhausted, I decided that wasn't reasonable at all so it couldn't possibly be God. And then I remembered that God once asked Gideon to reduce his army from thousands to three hundred, and then to lead it against a massive opposing army. Reasonable? Quite the opposite actually, so maybe it could be God.

A few minutes passed and I tried to read my Bible, but it looked like Chinese writing to me and I knew something wasn't right. So I packed up my stuff and turned to face a really steep hill a little ways in the distance. About an hour later I finally neared the top hoping to find the breeze that the mountain had blocked during my climb. My legs and arms were scratched from the thorn bushes I had to walk through, and my head pounded. I had stepped in cow manure crossing a pasture and trust me, the smell doesn't wear off in the grass as you walk! About that time I was thinking that leading an army of three hundred into battle sounded far more appealing than the climb I had just made. But then I took a few more steps and saw where I was.

The mountain spread out into a small plateau at the top and then formed a steep drop-off to sharp rocks below. Waves crashed powerfully upon the rocks. It was nothing like the peaceful shore where I had started, hoping to hear the soothing voice of God and not move for four hours. The waves displayed the wild, untamable power and fierceness of God's heart. And yet I found it more soothing at that moment than the waves creeping slowly up the sand. The wind blew strong across the top of the mountain and over me as I stood there. I thought that perhaps this was somewhat how Moses felt when he climbed up the mountain to meet God. Whether it was or not, I knew this was my Sanctuary, my resting place.

So far the stages of pursuing the dream have involved both internal and external challenges that probably have felt never-ending. You struggle to find the dream, only to be scared to death of doing it and have people tell you it's not a reasonable idea and you should just forget about it. And then after all that, you *still* haven't reached the dream but instead walk through a desert of tests and struggles.

A Breath of Fresh Air

When I first studied the stages of the dream, by the fourth one I had almost decided that I was not going to be a dreamer! I was close to filling out an application to be a McDonald's burger flipper on a 7 a.m.–5 p.m. schedule every single day for the rest of my life. But then I came across the fifth stage, Sanctuary. It was as if I was drowning under waters of fear, struggle, and pain, and then suddenly someone reached down and filled my lungs with air again. Sanctuary is that fresh breath of air that comes when we feel as if we can't keep going any longer.

Of the seven stages to the dream, Sanctuary is the

only optional phase. You can decide to go through it, avoid it, or go through only a little bit of it. It's entirely up to you. For once, no one can tell you what you should do. Great feeling, huh? But trust me on this one, you will regret it if you avoid it.

I've compared Sanctuary to a breath of fresh air, but what is it really? And no, it's not an oxygen mask that you can wear over your mouth and nose that breathes "dream thoughts" into your head (although that would be pretty cool). In order to enter this stage, WasteLand first has to end. So let's say that you've finally walked the entire length of the desert of preparation and suddenly all the sand disappears. Instead of plunging into the next stage, you come upon two signs pointing different directions. One says, "Sanctuary" and points left; the other says, "Continue the dream" and points forward. Sanctuary isn't a detour that takes you to the dream from another direction. It's not something you have to conquer in order to continue. Sanctuary is a time when God reaches down from heaven and invites you to draw near to Him and get to know His heart. It's a resting period before you go back to the journey to pursue the dream. His voice isn't loud when He invites you; it's more like a gentle soft tug at your heart. No one has to tell you that WasteLand is over, just like you can tell when a friend is no longer upset at you for missing the free throw that would have won the game. You just know that things are okay again. You can just tell. And the most amazing thing about WasteLand is that it's usually over when you think you can't go another step.

So here you are, faced with the decision either to stop and rest in a place called Sanctuary, or to continue your dream. To help you make a choice, let me put it into a little different perspective for you.

Rest and Rebuild

Imagine that it's 1750 and you're a big strong, muscular fighter. (Guys, I'm sure you'll have no problem picturing yourself this way; you probably do it every time you flex in front of the mirror. And girls, just think of the guy of your dreams in a suit of armor.) You've just returned from one of the most intense battles you've ever faced and haven't showered in weeks. Then again, I don't think they even had showers back then, so let's just say that you haven't been able to get in a river and wash the smell off. You're tired, but you won the battle! Inwardly you're pumped, but physically you're thinking you don't feel too much different than the guys you beat.

As soon as you enter the city gates, the trumpet sounds and a little short guy runs through the streets warning everyone in an annoyingly high-pitched voice, "Less than two days away is an enemy army from the west, and an even larger army is coming from the east in three weeks!" The captain of your army is a former captain of that large army coming from the east. He knows that the opposing army is strong and he knows intimately the tactics they use. He gets all his soldiers together, including you, and begins to walk through the ranks trying to decide who to send out to meet the immediate threat from the smaller enemy army and who to hold in reserve for a while. The ones who have just returned from battle are his strongest fighters and could quickly stop the attack of the smaller army from the west. But the attack that is three weeks away needs a strategic plan, not only skilled fighters. So what does he do?

You might not see how that story fits into this whole Sanctuary scene, so let me explain. We've already decided that you're a big, strong muscular fighter (I didn't think you'd appreciate it if I made you the little short guy who warns everyone in an annoying voice!) and you've just returned from the battle. You're tired and your strength is gone, but you're on a winning-streak high and you feel like you want to take out the rest of the bad men in the entire world. The Captain of the army is God, the Dream Giver. He's well aware of the situation, strategy, and strength needed to fight the large army, just as He knows the strength needed for you to fight what awaits you in the next stage of your pursuit of your dream. The Captain could tell you to just keep fighting even though you're exhausted and a smelly mess, but that wouldn't be a smart move on His part. Though you may want to keep going, physically and emotionally you need to stay. So He sends the rested ones into the battle nearing them in two days, and keeps back the ones who had just fought so they can rest and rebuild strength. Because He knows the opposing army intimately, He can instruct you best about how to defeat them. Who better to tell you than someone who knows their secrets?

But in real life, God doesn't make the decision whether or not you come into Sanctuary. It's your choice whether you rest and learn from Him as much as it is your choice whether you take a shower. But who better to tell you about your dream than the one who placed it in you? Who could know the intimate details of both you and your dream better than your Creator? And who could teach you best how to conquer the next phase than the one who knows everything? I think we have some pretty good reasons for staying for a while, don't you?

So, you look at the two signs and decide to head toward Sanctuary and to get back to "continuing the dream" a little later, when you're rested, informed, and know better the heart of the Creator of the dream. Now let's see what happens inside Sanctuary.

The Stages of Sanctuary

The first stage is to "come to the waters." It's a time of being comforted, strengthened, and restored from the sandblast experienced in the WasteLand. It's when your trust in God, which may have been tested in the WasteLand, is restored and He lets you see inside His heart as He heals yours. Perhaps you've experienced something like this already beneath a star-filled sky or during a worship time at a camp when God just seemed to envelop you in His arms. Each "come to the waters" experience is unique, but you always leave this stage closer to God and stronger (like that muscular warrior you were a few paragraphs ago).

The second stage is an invitation from God to "come into the light." One thing we know about God is that there is no imperfection in Him, whereas we are far from perfect…some days farther than others! But when He calls us into the light, His light shines into us and exposes all of our faults, flaws, and sins.

Doesn't sound too appealing, does it? The amazing thing about this stage is that though it scares us out of our minds to see what's inside us, we will desperately long to draw near to God here. The longing to walk closer to God's heart will be intense, and we can grow closer only when we look at the places in our heart that His light can't pass through and rid ourselves of them.

It's uncomfortable, I know. We've probably all been

at this stage at some point in our lives when we thought there couldn't possibly be anything else wrong with us, and then God opens our eyes to a whole new layer of flaws and imperfections. I remember a time when I felt pretty pathetic and thought, "This is never going to end. I'm hopeless!" But each time that God went deeper in probing my heart, He came closer. Little parts of us die inside, and when they do, that opens up space for Him to live in us. It's a painful but beautiful exchange.

The third and final stage is a plea to "come higher." When I was on the top of that mountain after being strengthened by the presence of God and spending time at His feet, my gaze suddenly lifted from what I was reading and I saw in the middle of a large, fenced-in pasture a pile of rocks. At any other time, I would have seen them as nothing more than rocks, but at that moment I knew that God had brought me up this mountain and before this pile of rocks for a reason. I knew that God was showing me an altar. The things He had revealed to me on that mountain needed to be sacrificed to Him—flaws, dreams, hopes, things I was holding on to too tightly, things I had never truly let go of. I hadn't known most of those things when I started up the mountain hours before. In fact I was completely shocked at some of the things He revealed that I hadn't been the least aware of before.

By this third stage, if you've decided to come this far in Sanctuary, your understanding and relationship with God will be tight. You'll know things about Him that you hadn't known before, and you'll see His heart in the most amazing way. He will gain your trust, and then He will ask you to use that trust and offer up to Him everything He has shown you.

And then comes the biggest, most difficult, and yet most appealing plea: "Will you give me your dream?" When God asked that of me, I thought for sure I was hearing the devil! God wouldn't ask me for my dream or ask me to move to Africa. I mean, *really*! Why would He possibly ask me to let go of my dream after He'd asked me to hold on to it so tightly and fight for it so hard?

When God asks us to let go of the dream, our first reflex is to tighten our hands around the dream and cry, "No!" By this stage, we've already sacrificed things for the dream and gone through so much junk and tests to get to this place that letting go seems like the most messed-up response possible. But God isn't asking us to end our pursuit of the dream. He's asking us to let Him hold the dream.

A Choice of Priority

You see, when we hold so tightly to the dream, we often unconsciously place the dream at a higher priority than the Dream Giver. During the first two stages of

Sanctuary, He lets us see more of Him and earns our trust so that when He asks us to let go, we'll know that His motives are pure. But letting go still seems like the hardest thing to do, and many people don't. They decide to leave Sanctuary with the dream still in their hands and go on to the next stage, but there's a danger to that, which we'll check out in the next chapter.

The choice whether or not to surrender the dream to His hands is yours. It is difficult, but make sure that you see the choice for what it is. It's a choice between whether you will value the dream more or value God more. It's a choice of priority. Though the dream is not bad, anything that takes the place of God in my priorities becomes an idol—no matter how innocent or good it may be.

This is the most amazing stage to me because it shows the jealous love of God for us. I hope that when you sit at the shore and hear Him calling you to go rest, to go deeper and higher, you will. It's never easy to let go of your dream. But when you do, it will bless His heart, and that's something you can never regret.

Just wait and see

And you won't be disappointed with what He does with it.

Just wait and see!

In order to **change** the way we **live**,
we **have to** change the
way we **think**

land of giants:
why they don't just choke on flies
and die

Have you ever wondered why God didn't just
miraculously kill Goliath while he was asleep instead of
having David hurl a rock at him? (I must admit, though,
that was a pretty cool way to do it.) I mean, God is all-
powerful so it wouldn't have been difficult for Him to just
have the giant choke on a fly while he snored. But could it
be that God had a bigger plan and deeper intentions for
using David the way He did?

I'm sure most of you know at least one person whose
perspective on life has a negative effect on everything they
do and say. Maybe one of the guys on your basketball
team thinks he's God's gift to women and goes on and on
about how all he has to do is smile and they're captivated

for the rest of their lives. Or maybe he sees himself as the best athlete on the team and drives the rest of the team crazy because he acts like he's the only player on the floor. We've all met people like this and probably have become a little frustrated when their wrong perspective caused wrong behavior.

Perspective is what makes us live the way we do

Perspective is what makes us live the way we do. If our perspective is that success and money are the most important things, we'll probably seek out a high-paying career and become a doctor, lawyer, or business executive. If our perspective is happiness oriented, we'll probably not look first at how much a job pays but whether or not we'll love it every day of our lives.

Perspective affects everything—our goals, lifestyle, friendships, priorities. So when our perspective is off, it affects us whether we realize it or not. In order to change the way we live, we have to change the way we think. But if we don't know that our perspective is wrong, we'll just keep walking down our present path. Maybe your perspective on giants isn't wrong. But I know mine was for a while, and it affected a lot of areas of my life I wish it hadn't.

So, what needs to change about our perception of giants? Why did God use David, the most unlikely giant killer, instead of just knocking Goliath over Himself? And what exactly *are* the giants we face in our journey toward our dream? Let's answer that question first, and then we'll come back to the "why?" and "what needs to change?" questions.

Obstacles to Your Dream

Giants are external obstacles that stand in the way of you and your dream *after* you have begun to pursue it. Though you may already know some giants you will face if you pursue your dream (such as having to raise money for a mission trip, sports camp, or even just to buy a car), you'll actually face those giants only after you actively begin to do things to make your dream a reality.

Giants are pretty intimidating to even look at, much less fight. If I were to meet a WWE wrestler, I would definitely be intimidated; but if I were put in a ring with him, I would be scared out of my mind! Some giants make us feel like the smallest and weakest person on earth with no ability to change things. But we can overcome them. We can change them. And we can reach our dreams. *We just have to want it bad enough and fight for it hard enough.* Here are a few universal and well-known giants. See if any of them are familiar:

♣ *People who stand between you and your dream.* Perhaps
someone has the ability to help you with your
dream, but that person either doesn't want to help
or actively opposes you and your dream.

♣ *Cultural norms.* I believe this is one of the most
intimidating giants facing teenagers today. Almost
every dream God gives us is completely
unsupported by the world. Let's say your dream is to
start your own business and run it with all the
integrity you can. Looking around, it's hard to find
more than a handful of businesses like that. Most
are concerned only with making a profit and staying
on top, not at all concerned with pleasing God.

♣ *Past mistakes or circumstances.* Perhaps your past
mistakes have let people down, and asking them to
trust you again when you pursue this dream seems
almost like asking them to catch the moon and give
it to you. You'll have to fight just to gain their trust
in areas where you may not have been trustworthy
before. Circumstances can also be a giant opposing
dreams. One of the hardest things about being a
teenager with a dream is that you are controlled a
lot by what your parents decide *for* you. You
probably don't have much say about whether your
dad or mom take the job offer in Los Angeles or
what occupation they are in. Maybe even the well-
known giant of divorce stands in the way, mockingly

telling you that you will turn out just like your parents did: "You'll never reach your dream of having a strong, godly marriage. Just read the divorce statistics. Look at your own parents! What more proof do you need? Your dream to have a God-centered marriage is impossible and foolish. All you'll ever do is fight and be miserable. So why even try?"

❧ *Money and personal challenges.* Money is another big giant. College and a career you want to follow may seem impossible because your family will never have enough money to support you. Challenges such as a troubled family life, tragedy, illness, and physical disabilities can also be giants that hit you and your dream so hard that you think there's no way you can reach it now.

I think most teenagers can recognize at least one of those giants opposing their dream, though you may face different ones depending on your particular dream. I talked with a friend in Cape Town the other day whose professional rugby career had been put on hold because he tore some ligaments in his leg. He was beginning to think he was never going to reach his goals. But regardless of the giant, it's important to know that every dream has giants and that you aren't the only one who has to face them. We can't reach our dream without at least a little struggle.

Though these giants are pretty discouraging and seem, at times, to be stronger than your dream, the One who created and placed that dream inside of you is so much stronger than the giants will ever be. As the saying goes, "Don't tell God how big the storm is in your life; tell the storm how big the God is in your life." You can rise above cultural norms, mistakes, circumstances, and people's opinions of you. Finding yourself facing opposition to your dream doesn't necessarily mean that God is telling you to back off and stop chasing your dream. Amazingly enough, God wants you to keep going and defeat these giants, because not only does it help you reach your dream, it also helps Him.

Bringing Glory to God

Let's go back to the story of David. Goliath has just crashed to the ground, and the people are going crazy, screaming and shouting. Israel experienced greater freedom, the nation was introduced to its next king, but most of all, praises to God rang out through the entire country and He was honored. Though praises would have been lifted no matter *how* Goliath died, they were lifted *to God* when it was evident that God's hand had intervened on David's behalf. When the people looked at this puny boy and the massive dead giant, I don't think anyone had to tell them that God had done something awesome. I'm pretty sure they put that one together.

A friend of mine told me that God never asks crazy and unobtainable things of us. He asks us to do small things that we are capable of and then to just have faith that He will take care of the rest. All God asked David to do was to hurl a rock in the air; He would bring the giant down. He asked Moses to simply raise a staff; God took it from there and parted the waters. All Peter did was walk (nothing impossible), and God took the water beneath his feet and held him up. God will take those small things and our faith and make something amazing that will bring glory to Him.

Giants are opportunities for us to bring glory to God. By defeating them in such a way that people can't help but see the hand of God, He is glorified. The bigger the giant, the more glory God receives and the more His name is praised. Running from the giant because we are intimidated also means that we are running from the chance to have others praise God when they see how He delivers us. Giants may seem big and undefeatable to us, but beside God they are so small you can barely see them. It's all about having the correct perspective.

Unlike border bullies, the threats of giants are not always exaggerated. I'm sure many of you know the story about the twelve spies Moses sent into Canaan to check out the land and report back what they saw. Ten came back describing the situation as it was. The army was trained well, giants were in the land, and they didn't think they had a chance. Two spies came with reports of faith, knowing that the God who had parted the Red Sea could handle the giants, and also knowing that He would get praise because of it. But Israel decided not to rely on faith, and because of that they walked in circles in the sand for *forty years!* And guess what? Forty years later, when they finally were ready to cross the Jordan River to enter the land of promise, the giants were still there. But this time Israel had faith, relied on God, and brought the giants down!

Giants present risks, yes. You can get hurt. Some only stand in the way, but some will actively fight you and your dream until either your dream or the giant is overcome. None are as big as the God who put the dream in you in the first place. You can overcome challenges and obstacles— you can reach your dream—but only if you go toward the giants and not away from them. And trust me, if you wait until they are gone, you will be old and toothless and never have reached your dream. But the saddest thing of all will be that God will not have been glorified because you didn't choose to have faith.

One of the most amazing verses for overcoming giants is found in 2 Chronicles: "The eyes of the LORD run to and fro throughout the whole earth, to show Himself strong on behalf of those whose heart is loyal to Him." Never again run away from giants. Challenges are only opportunities in disguise! They can be overcome; your dream can be reached.

God wants to use you, and He deserves all the glory.

Challenges are only **opportunities** in **disguise**

God is **using** you to **accomplish** His dream that He **placed** in you

CHAPTER SEVEN

land of promise:
embarrassing moments and
star-filled nights

Have you ever had a picture in your mind about what something was going to be like, only to have it turn out nothing like that? When I was younger and first started playing basketball, in my mind I was Michael Jordan. The only problem was that I was the exact opposite in every way possible—I was a little white girl who didn't have any moves at all! In my mind I pictured screaming fans as I dunked the basketball and our team defeated the other school's team by two hundred points (or something ridiculous like that). Well, the game didn't go quite as I had imagined. We ended up losing, and I think our parents cringed more than they cheered. One of my teammates even scored on the wrong goal. That was one of the first times I realized that our hopes don't always match up with reality. And unfortunately I was reminded of that again just a few months ago.

I had flown down to Cape Town to spend a week with friends and went out one night with another friend who lived in the area. I had hoped for a fun evening, and it was. I just hadn't expected the embarrassing disaster that accompanied it.

It got to be pretty late, and I and the friend I was with (I'll call him Colin) decided it was time for him to drop me off at the house where I was staying. Unfortunately, everyone in the house was asleep and didn't hear their cell phones ringing when I called to get directions. I had no idea where the house was from where we were. I was randomly making up directions as Colin drove along, telling him "turn right" or "turn left," pretending I had even the slightest idea how to get to where we needed to go.

About forty-five minutes later I recognized the gate to the house and told Colin to stop. I got out and looked up at the big wall in front of the house. I had no key, so I tried once again to wake someone with my cell phone. When that didn't work, I decided I would just have to scale the wall. So I jumped up, grabbed on to the top of the wall, and pulled myself over. Looking completely unladylike and I'm sure absolutely hilarious (I could tell Colin was trying hard not to laugh and actually look concerned), I swung my leg over and suddenly heard a *rrrriiiippp.* I looked down to see that my skirt had split all the way up the front.

Holding my skirt together as best I could, I finally was able to wake one of my friends up to let me in the house. All of this while Colin stood watching, and who knows what he was thinking.

Needless to say, the night had gone nothing like I had hoped, and though Colin was a complete gentleman through it all, I couldn't have been more mortified. I hoped that perhaps I would wake up the next morning and discover it had all been a dream.

Matching Hopes with Reality

Unfortunately, situations like this—where the details of life don't exactly match my expectations—happen often to me. So I've learned not to be too surprised when things turn out different than I had anticipated. Nevertheless, I found myself shocked and taken aback when I entered one of my first Lands of Promise.

It was the middle of the night Atlanta time when my family and I landed in Johannesburg, South Africa, and yet the sun was just rising there. It seemed to mock me as it rose knowing full well that I had no ability to change anything. But I knew that we had gone through comfort zones, border bullies, struggle and testing to get here, and a part of me was excited about this missionary experience we were stepping into. And yet another part of me ached over what I was leaving behind.

We got a cart for all of our suitcases—three pieces of luggage each, the only belongings we brought with us. On our way from the airport I looked out the window, and I remember thinking that this Land of Promise couldn't be further from what I had pictured. Instead of being filled with hope at actively beginning to do the dream of helping the people here, a sickening feeling filled my heart and soul. Women with small children were at every street corner begging for food or money. Thousands of shacks made from scraps of metal were the scenery that continued on as far as the eye could see. This was not what I expected when I thought about doing my dream.

The dream that first caused my heart to sing was a picture of the need *fulfilled.* It was a picture of myself with people well, happy, and helped. It's this kind of picture that will lead you through all the stages of your dream. But this picture is what it should look like *after you've realized your dream,* not what it looks like before you even start.

When I picture my dream of purity before marriage, I picture the look on my husband-to-be's face as I walk down the aisle, knowing that he is the one I waited for. I don't picture all the struggles along the way and all the possible loneliness from staying true to my standards. When little boys picture being professional football players, they picture stadiums filled with screaming fans. They never think about the torturous training and demanding workouts. When a person dreams of becoming a teacher, she thinks about a classroom of well-behaved kids, not about the years of studying she has to go through to get to that place. The picture is the dream lived out, not how we got there. But that's the most important part of the journey of our dream.

Pretend that your dream is an island, and on a bright summer day you board a boat that will take you there. You look through a telescope and can see the island far, far on the horizon. The island is tropical and happy children are playing on the white beaches. And then you back away from the telescope and squint into the distance. The island looks nothing like it did in the telescope. No sandy white beaches, no green lush trees, and from what you can tell, the children look far from happy. The magic telescope gives you a picture of the dream completed, but with the naked eye, the island you are headed toward looks nothing like that close-up view. But as you keep moving toward it, eventually it will. It's a dream waiting for you to make it reality.

Most people think that when they enter the Land of Promise they'll be able to just sit down and chill out for a while. Usually, though, they learn quickly enough that just arriving in the Land of Promise doesn't mean that their dream is done. It means that finally they are able to *do* the

dream. And usually God has a little more in mind than
we thought.

Finding that out, however, is nothing like the feeling
you get when you discover that an assignment you've been
given will require a lot more work than you first
anticipated. Remember, you are created to love your
dream and to become alive and so amazingly fulfilled in
doing it.

Expanding Your Dream

What often happens after you've been in the Land of
Promise for a while is that God asks you to do a little
more and fulfill a little more of the dream. Perhaps you're
wondering why He didn't show you in the beginning
everything He desired you to do. It's probably because we
wouldn't be able to handle it. The dream already seemed
impossible when we started. But somehow we've made it,
it's become possible, and God wants to expand it just a
little more.

When He begins to expand your dream, He usually
starts by changing your mind-set from "What can I do?"
to "What does God want done?" From our human
perspective, we look at things with all of our fears,
insecurities, and weaknesses instead of looking at them
with faith in God's power. And often our thoughts about

what needs to be done are far from what God knows needs to be done.

By this stage, God has taken you a long way. You've gone through more than you ever dreamed possible when you were sitting in that comfort zone with your dreams safely tucked away in your heart and doing nothing about them. You've gone through tests, attacks, and so much more, and through all that, He has proven Himself faithful and able to do what seemed impossible to you. God doesn't usually ask you to do something extraordinary until He's shown Himself faithful to you. He builds up your trust in Him, and then He asks you to trust Him even more, knowing that you have no reason not to except for your fear of looking like a fool. But it's often in those times when we look like a fool that God is glorified the most.

If you aren't willing to be thought foolish for God, then you have a long way to go in dealing with your fear of others. Though no one ever says, "Oh, I'm so excited! I'm going to look like a fool today for God! It's going to be so much fun!" your willingness to recklessly abandon yourself to God—to be willing to do what He asks without questioning why—is beautiful in His sight. It's like Joshua instructing the people to blow those trumpets until the walls fall down and not being able to explain to his troops why exactly they were to do this except that "God said so."

The Land of Promise is the most selfless stage of the dream because instead of you holding on to the dream for your reasons or sharing it with God just a little, it becomes God using you to accomplish His dream that He placed in you. It's one of the most rewarding and fulfilling feelings ever.

Starting Over Again

So here you are, standing in the Land of Promise with God expanding your dream. You're living it out daily, looking around and wondering what on earth comes next. Suddenly you realize that the things you're doing now would have scared you to death when you were in the Land of Familiar at the beginning of your dream. Now they don't scare you at all and you're pretty *comfortable*. And then *wham!* another dream comes like a bug hitting your windshield. And it's right in front of your face! You can look around it or under it, and if you were going fast enough when it hit, maybe even *through* it, but it's still there. And guess what? You're right back where you started!

Now, I'm not saying that your comfort zone has shrunk all the way down to the size it was when you first started your dream. It's still the same size as you stretched

> The Land of Promise is the most selfless stage of the dream

it out to be in order to meet the dream. But you're back at the very beginning of the journey in the "dream stage," only this time your heart is holding a whole new dream. And this time, the dream is a little bigger than before, because you're starting with an already stretched comfort zone.

Think about it like this: you buy one of those little kiddie pools (not for yourself, I hope) and start blowing it up. After about thirty minutes you're feeling light-headed, so you put in the plug, take a break, and then come back in a while to blow it up some more. You don't start at the very beginning again because all of that air you blew in is still in there. You start where you left off and blow it up bigger.

Apply that example to your dream. The blow-up pool is your comfort zone. The first dream you had blew it up a little bit and stretched it out. And then you took a break and kept going through the next stages until you got to the Land of Promise. After a while, the Land of Promise becomes your *new* Land of Familiar, your new comfort zone. The next dream that comes along is outside of this comfort zone that has already been blown up a little. So to pursue and live out this bigger dream, you have to go back and add some more air and expand the new comfort zone. Each dream starts *outside* the comfort zone you were in when you finished the previous dream.

And so, the journey of the dream starts all over

again—if you let it, that is! The new dream will make you enlarge your comfort zone even more. Border bullies will stand at the BorderLand and tell you to go back as they did before. Some of the border bullies will be the same; some will be new. The WasteLand will be just as dry and sandy, and yet this time you'll understand more of why you're there. Sanctuary will present that soft whisper from the heart of God telling you to come to the waters, into the light, and to climb higher with this new dream in your heart. Giants will try to kill the dream again, whether by force or by passive resistance. The Land of Promise will be there waiting at the end, and God will be right there walking with you every step of the way—from the moment He puts the dream in you until you stand on the soft grass of the Land of Promise. He's there in Sanctuary when He wraps His arms around you and feels closer to you than the air you breathe. Even in WasteLand, during those moments when He feels farther than the moon, He's still there. The One who placed that dream in you will never leave you. Ever.

Made to Dream

Life is made up of dream after dream after dream. Each dream gets bigger, and each one brings more glory to God. If you never follow your first dream, you'll never find the bigger dreams that await you after that first one is done. You'll simply remain in the small comfort zone that the first dream asks you to break out of. (Though, I must admit, comfort zones never feel very small when you're trying to break out of them. Remember, no matter how big your comfort zone is, it will still be uncomfortable to move.)

Each dream is in your hands to chase, forsake, ignore, or weaken. Yes, a dreamless life is much less risky. You won't meet any border bullies because there'll be no reason for them to stop you. You won't ever shake anything if you don't move. Giants won't oppose you because there won't be any dream to stop. But your heart will cry itself to sleep at night, begging you to follow your dream just once and see what happens. God will whisper to you in the stillness of the day, "You were made for more than this!" You were made by Him *to dream*.

A few weeks ago I sat underneath a star-filled sky just "being still and knowing that He is God." I was struggling with a few things as I looked up at the inky vastness, feeling so small and lost in it. My eyes scanned the sky until they locked on one particularly bright star that I was unable to look away from. It was brighter than all the other stars. It wasn't in a cluster of stars but was by itself. God quietly whispered to my heart, "Though at times standing alone can feel like the loneliest, most painful place to be, those who stand alone capture and hold My gaze. The ones who are okay with being different and shining brighter are the ones I can't look away from. Don't try to be like everyone else when you were meant to stand apart. Don't kill the dreams that set you apart and make you different, for your dreams make you who you are."

I may not ever meet you, but I hope with all my heart that someday I hear about you and your pursuit and achievement of a seemingly impossible dream. I hope that you decide to chase your dreams and abandon comfort. I hope you decide to listen to your heart and the One who created you more than you listen to people bent on discouraging you from pursuing your dream. But most of all, I hope that you *live* instead of only dreaming *about* living.

May the God of all your dreams look upon you and see a passionate dream seeker daily living to bring Him glory. May your dreams be not only "wishes upon stars," but may they be your *life*.

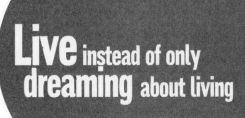

Live instead of only dreaming about living

Are You Living Your Dream?
Or Just Living Your Life?

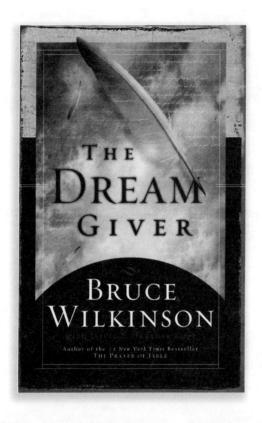

Your life dream is the key to God's greatest glory and your greatest fulfillment. There's no limit to what He can accomplish if you wholeheartedly pursue your created purpose! Let Bruce Wilkinson show you how to rise above the ordinary, conquer your fears, and overcome the obstacles that keep you from living your Big Dream.

ISBN 1-59052-201-X
$16.99

THE DREAM GIVER SERIES

THE DREAM GIVER FOR COUPLES
Let Bruce and Darlene Marie Wilkinson take you on a journey that will give you hope as you discover the seven principles to experiencing the marriage you've always dreamed of.

ISBN 1-59052-460-8

THE DREAM GIVER FOR TEENS
It's time to begin the journey of your life. Let Bruce and Jessica Wilkinson help you find your dream and pursue it on a quest to discover the life you've always dreamed of.

ISBN 1-59052-459-4

THE DREAM GIVER FOR PARENTS
In this practical guide, Bruce and Darlene Marie share with you the seven secrets for guiding your children to discover and pursue their Dreams.

ISBN 1-59052-455-1

The Dream Giver
Multimedia Resources
from

*I*n this 8-part seminar taught by Bruce Wilkinson, you are invited to follow your heart and find your destiny in an inspired Life Dream that is uniquely yours.

- ■ **Ideal for Sunday School, Small Groups, or Personal Study**
- ■ **Available in DVD, VHS, and Audio CD and Cassettes**
- ■ **Study Guides are available for group studies**
- ■ **Use the audio series to learn while you drive**

Also included as a special feature on the DVD and VHS set, hear interviews with Rick Warren, John Tesh, Robert Schuller, George Forman, Kirk Cameron, and Delilah.

for more information please visit:

www.thedreamgiver.com
www.brucewilkinson.com

The Dream Assessment

*A*re you excited about your Dream Journey, but aren't sure where to start? DISC and the Dream Assessment will give you the tools you need to pursue and achieve your Big Dream.

Once you've taken DISC, a Dream Assessment is instantly customized for you based on your personality type. Everyone approaches the Dream Journey differently, and you have a unique way of pursuing your Dreams! Discover more about each stage of your Dream and how you handle the challenges along the way.

for more information please visit:

www.thedreamgiver.com